William Henry Holmes

Palenque, Mexico, 1895

William Henry Holmes

Palenque, Mexico, 1895

ISBN/EAN: 9783743464995

Manufactured in Europe, USA, Canada, Australia, Japa

Cover: Foto ©ninafisch / pixelio.de

Manufactured and distributed by brebook publishing software (www.brebook.com)

William Henry Holmes

Palenque, Mexico, 1895

Sut floor 3rd from lith

N

$$\frac{\begin{array}{r}36\\20\end{array}}{56}$$

height of this story about 4 [?].
doors 6 in deep,
[illegible] west & prob. 2
originally., prob same + ant,

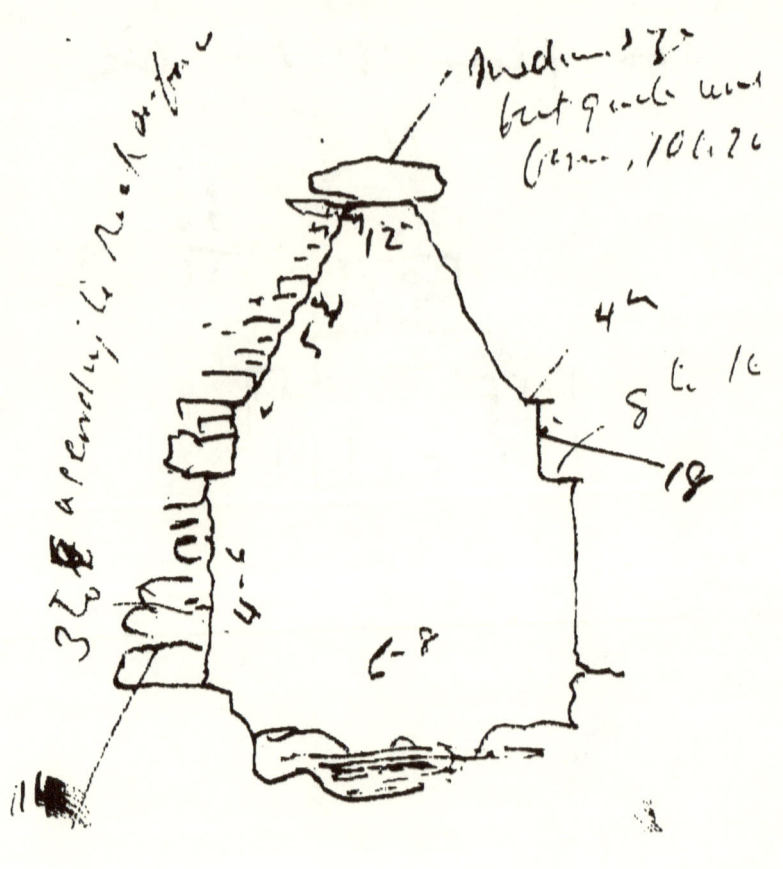

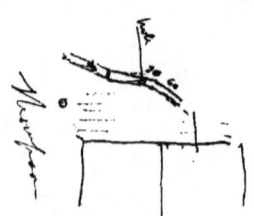

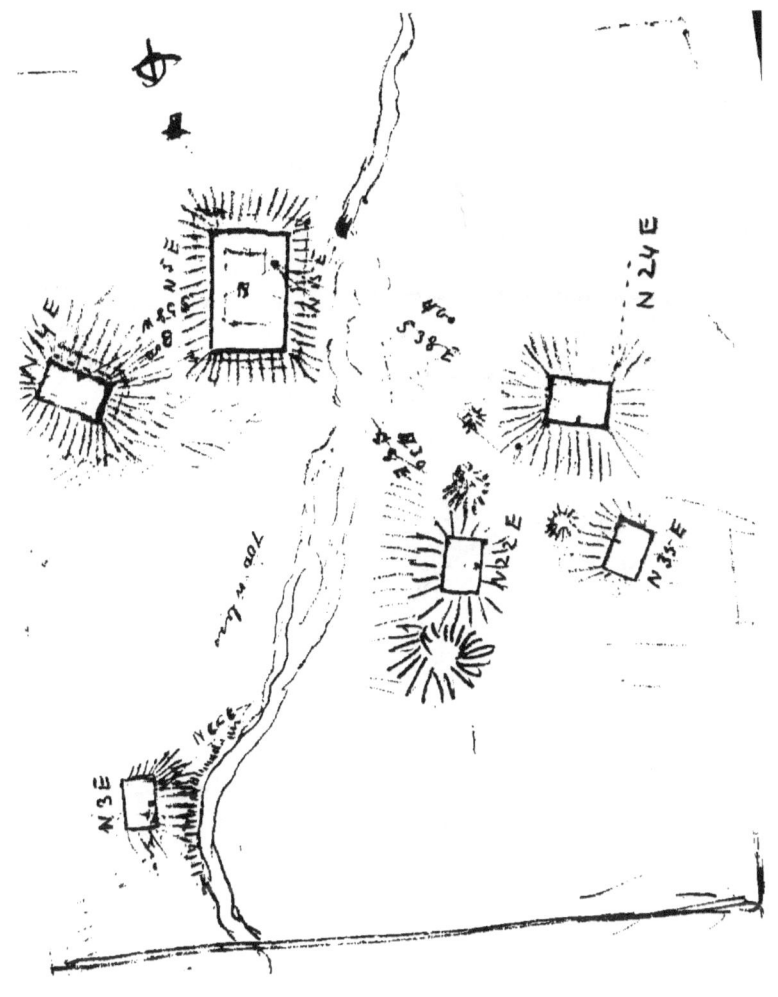

Tottering top of ft above upper step at north. This stair represents the level of the floor of this upper story as does the one below on the south side. As in the case below it is written about 3 ft of the outer edge of the wall

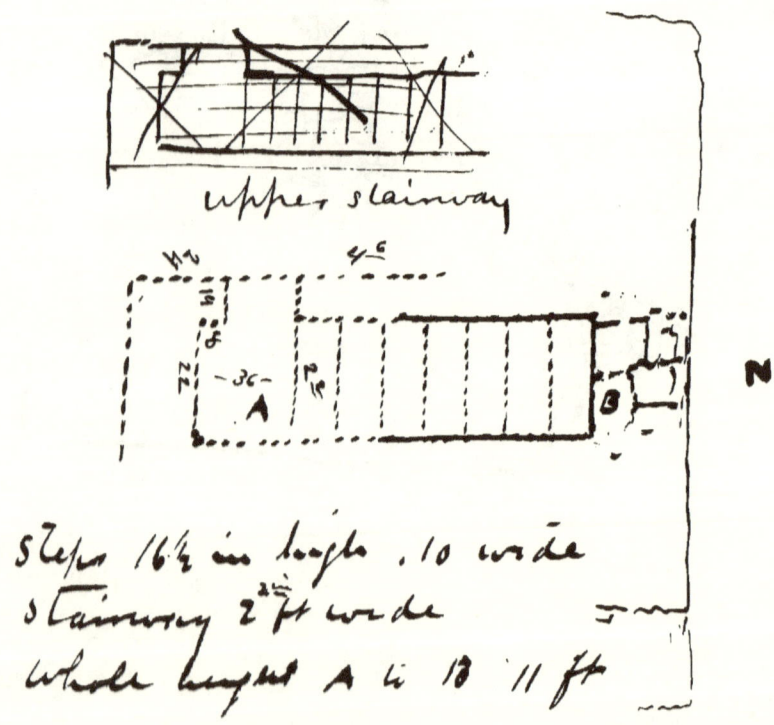

Steps 16½ in length, 10 wide
Stairway 2¼ ft wide
Whole height A to B 11 ft

Square tower, 3 stories over a ground floor ornamented to the north with pointed arches (wrong)

Top story some (fallen in partly) not unlike the corral ales lower decorations — not so rich

Picture p. 241

Function of palace & city.
Judgery sculptures &c
          Charnay p 246

Descriptive texts

Aqueduct. Covered Canal

p 229

and pass up the right bank
of a small tributary to the
Chefboundary, of the entry half a
mile up. The ascent is by
slight slopes through the
forest and over walls & scatter
heaps of stones however at
the left beneath we hear the

fully as the water charges with
liquid from the table and
runs above that everything
it touches is cooled & slow
and shells fruits & even
legs are rapidly deeply
cooled so as to seem wet.
repead.

of the palace. the stream 40 ft away issues here from an arched way and rattles down the rocky bed. ~~the point of view for my miniature panorama, which as in other cases I have designed as a sort of key, is assumed to be~~ ~~taken from a point of view assumed to be some 20 or ft vertically over this point.~~ We climbed to the palace at the right. the great courtyard quadrangle pile in the foreground & for the

dense forest of the bas
y the steeper slopes
The great hall of the palace
The three tablets
The Bean relief on same side
of stream. The cross, the sun
of the cross Temple. others obscure
Point out all six
Describe all in detail omitting
what others have & will cover
Special topics. sculpt. paint, &c
Close with description of city
& culture.

Palenque 8

with stucco. The walls were
roughly faced up with the
purpose of making the applica-
tion of stucco easy and per-
manent. Cut ^a dressed faces were
not required. The walls of
the towers are a good example
of the carrying up of walls
with smallish stones & flags
only evenly laid in mortar
the plaster now been to a
great extent fallen off.

It was probably very diffi-
cult to secure large stones
and curiously enough the

The quarries have not been discovered, the tablets seem different & may have had a distant origin. The local rock is not of good texture generally and is much changed and crated.

Vast bodies of mortar & stucco were used and it is not to be supposed for a moment that any other material than lime burned from the ever present limestone was used, shells plentiful but the body not sufficient. It would seem

The deposits by percolating water. Slalop & coatings. The solidifying of walls

Building of bases for slice work. Combs on roofs, &c.

Color Palenque

Color was lavishly and there is no reason to doubt carefully used by the people of Palenque. Black, white, blue, two reds — a dark and an orange or sienna red — yellow and green. The *approximately* same scale used elsewhere in Mexico and Central America.

The plaster and stucco was white and some walls, ceilings and other surfaces were left — the plain color but it would

seems that not only the show
spaces but obscure surfaces
were carefully tinted and that
even the outside walls and roofs
received color finish many if not all in cases.

As time or use injured the
colored surfaces other applications
were made and it is not
uncommon to find traces in the
broken sections of plaster of six
or more successive coats more
or less deeply buried by renewed
applications of plaster or wash
of plain color.

Color was also used in decorating
the walls in various designs

Color 3

geometric, pictorial and in the nature of picture writing and glyphs, and traces are seen in numerous protected places. The most elaborate and showy work was in the painting of the stucco figures and groups with which all parts of the buildings were embellished. The colors as they stand today are often bright and pleasing, and it is a most remarkable fact that on surfaces fully exposed to the elements and to the destructive agencies of vegetable and animal life for 400 years or more these tints (colors) are still well preserved.

The painting of the figures, mostly life size or colossal and in middle or high relief was no doubt conventional following perhaps the styles employed in painting the skin &c but it is observed that as a rule the flesh is red — a rather pale tint and that this tune took the whole scale. It is apparent that the distribution and effect of color in these subjects

Color 5

was in general the same as that seen in kindred subjects seen in ancient Mex. Manuscripts — such is published in Kingsborough.

Of the nature and composition of the colors little can be made out with certainty. The sienna red — used in all Aztec Toltec and Maya countries — is thought to be of vegetable origin, to have been produced from the red wood of the — — tree. Common throughout the various states

The blue — —

We scaled without a ladder passing around to the south a large tree with crawling braces was found growing on the corner of the pyramid and almost touching the wide eave stones above. The trunk was smooth but the vines were strong and a few moments hard work found me on the roof which ascended with alternate slopes and shelves in some six increments to the base of the roof crest. The section of the whole

FIELD COLUMBIAN MUSEUM
CHICAGO.

sufficient reason for its elaboration. There are three ideas to be suggested ① a natural apex to the roof, ② developed as an outlook, ③ elaborated for beauty. The first will not be sufficient to account for this growth, the second suggests a function incongruous with the uses of a temple & besides no sufficient provision is apparent for convenient ascent from below. The Aesthetic function deserves full consideration, but here as elsewhere

FIELD COLUMBIAN MUSEUM
CHICAGO.

strange stone work frame was built to support sculptures which while heavy — were wonderfully effective from the aesthetic point of view were also religious in character & topic and we cannot say how essential these figures in this position & this relation to the things below & those above was to the builders.

That the entire surface of these structures was covered with

FIELD COLUMBIAN MUSEUM
CHICAGO.

seem a little against reason & common sense to place works intended to please the eye and the eye alone where that could not be seen with advantage from any possible point of view.

Construction
Details of placing
Sculpture

FIELD COLUMBIAN MUSEUM
CHICAGO.

As to the construction of the tomb or crest it is simple and easily understood. The roof of the Sura affords a level space 8 × 32 feet which serves to support two parallel walls running the whole length, 2 ft thick each at the base and separated by a four foot space, the walls as the ascend incline inward at an angle of two or 3 degrees and at the height of eight feet are joined by an arch of the usual type, the covering in the interspace making a gallery and on the arch is pleasantly is built — all is built of small stones & flags laid in [order?] and faced with

FIELD COLUMBIAN MUSEUM
CHICAGO.

plaster

The feature that attracts first attention is the perforation of the walls.

Construction details

Firmness; lightness
  Openness

? Yet another idea makes it apparent that neither of these may have been preponderant. The primary object was to secure a support for sculpture

FIELD COLUMBIAN MUSEUM
CHICAGO.

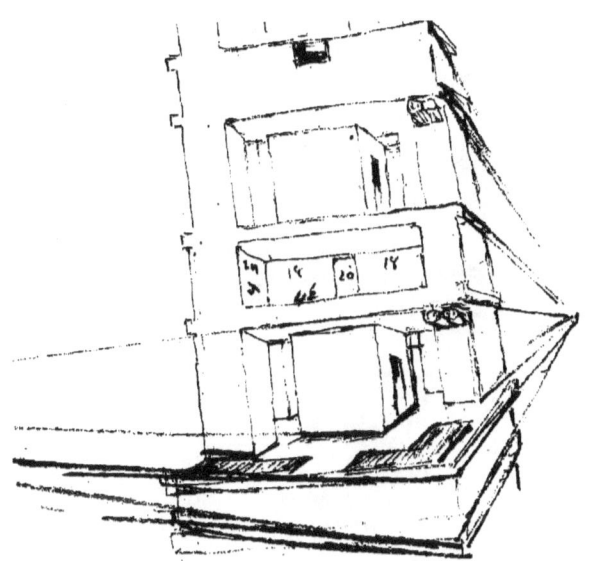

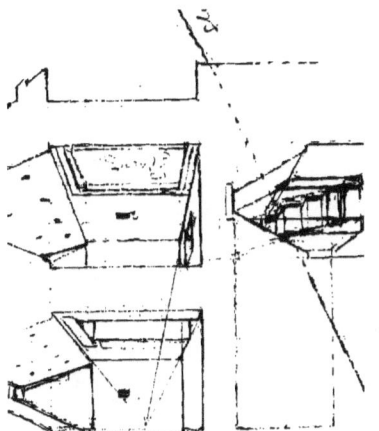

2

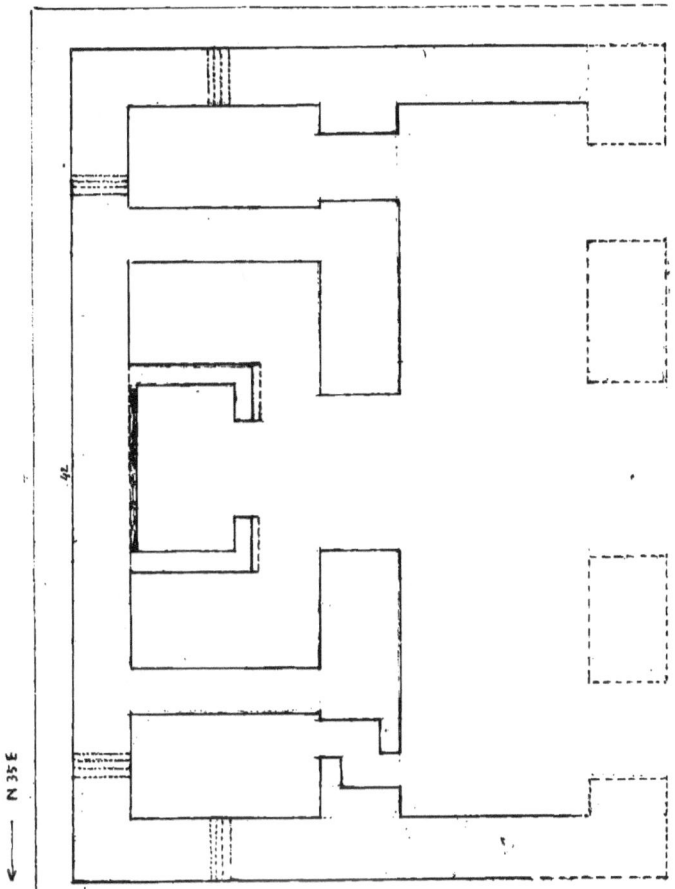

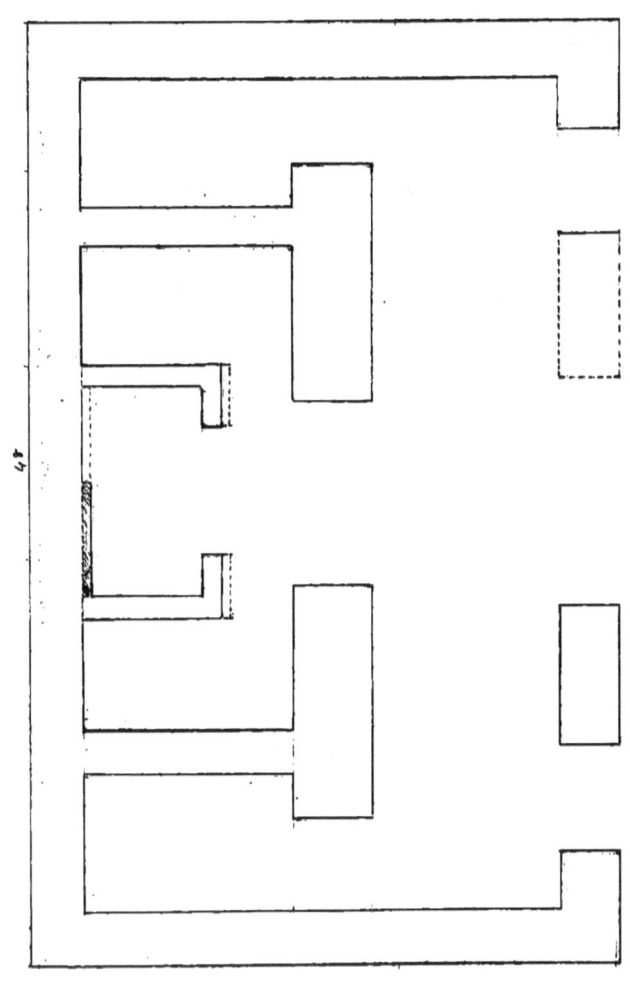

6

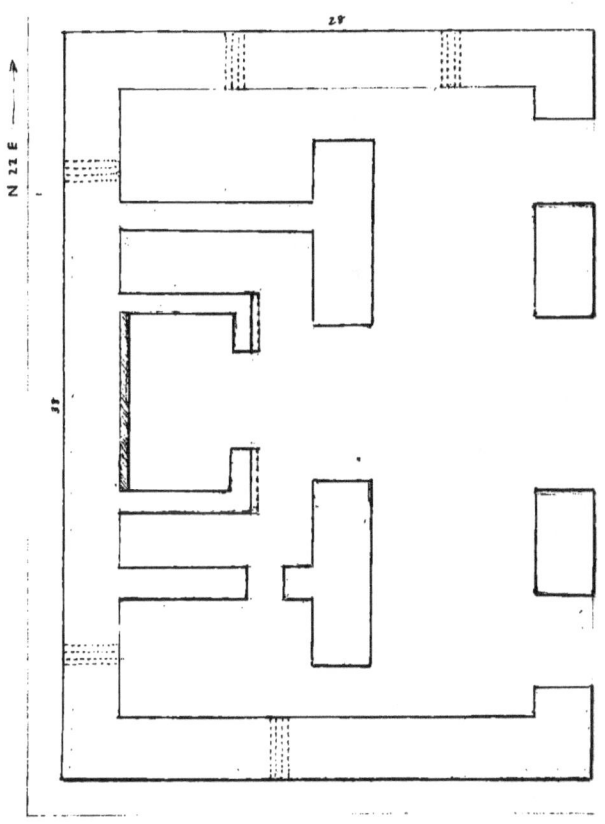

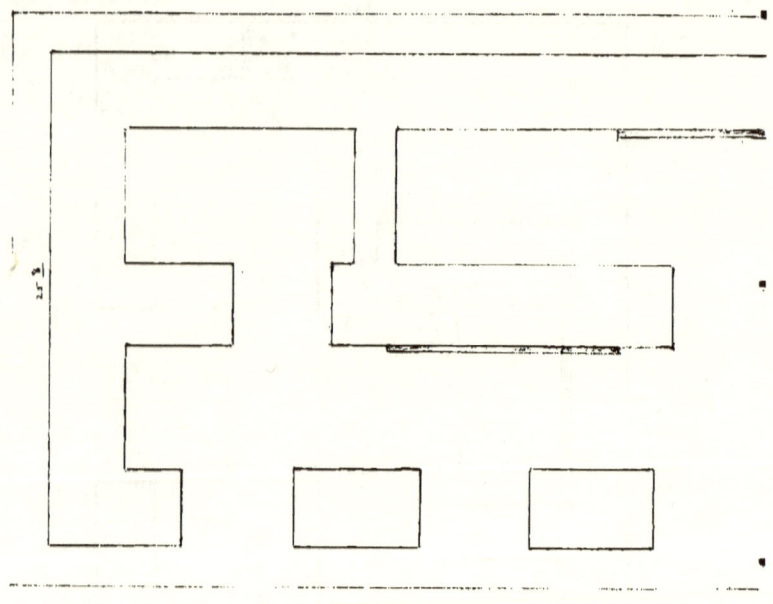

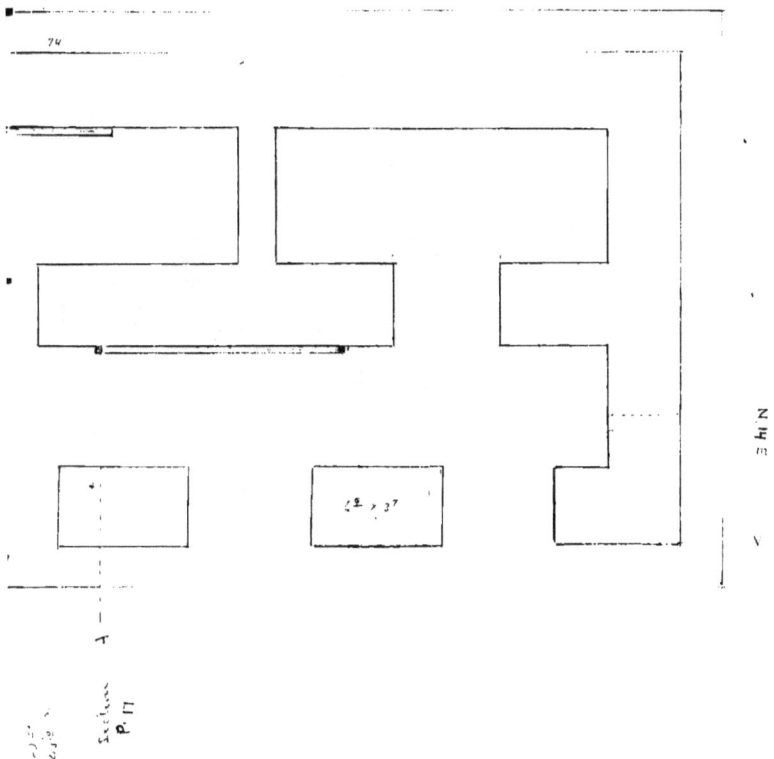

10

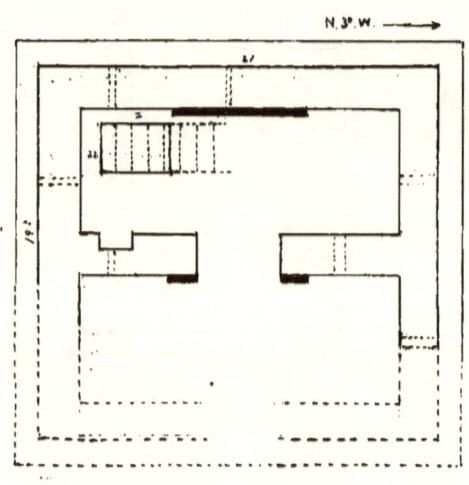

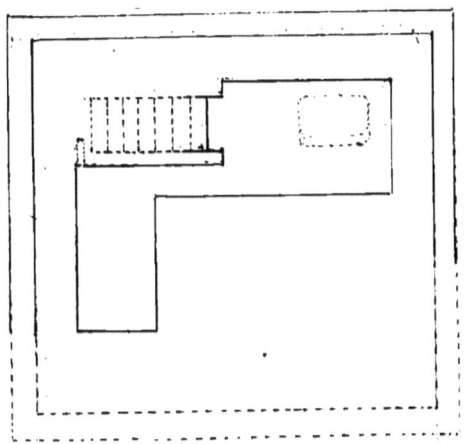

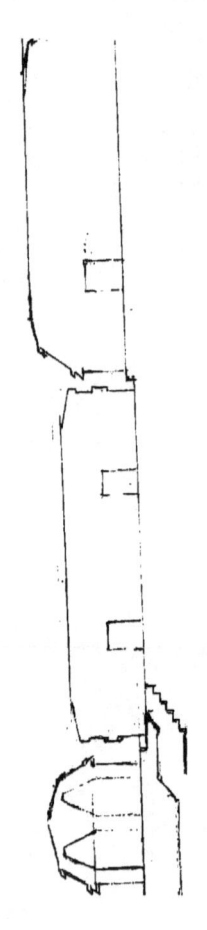

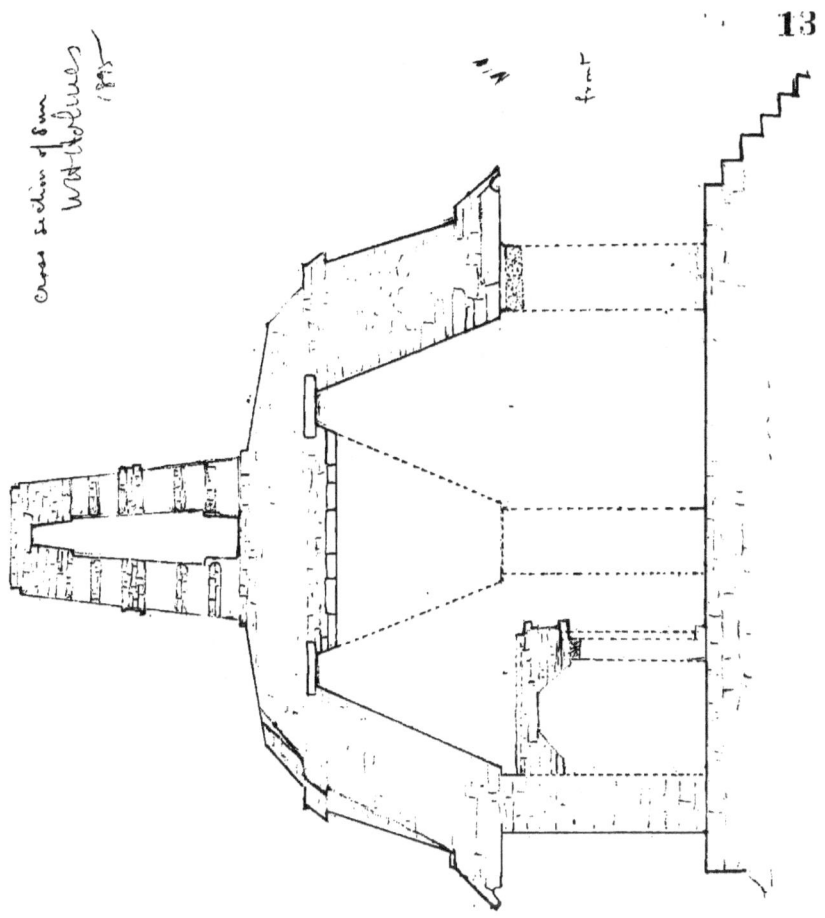

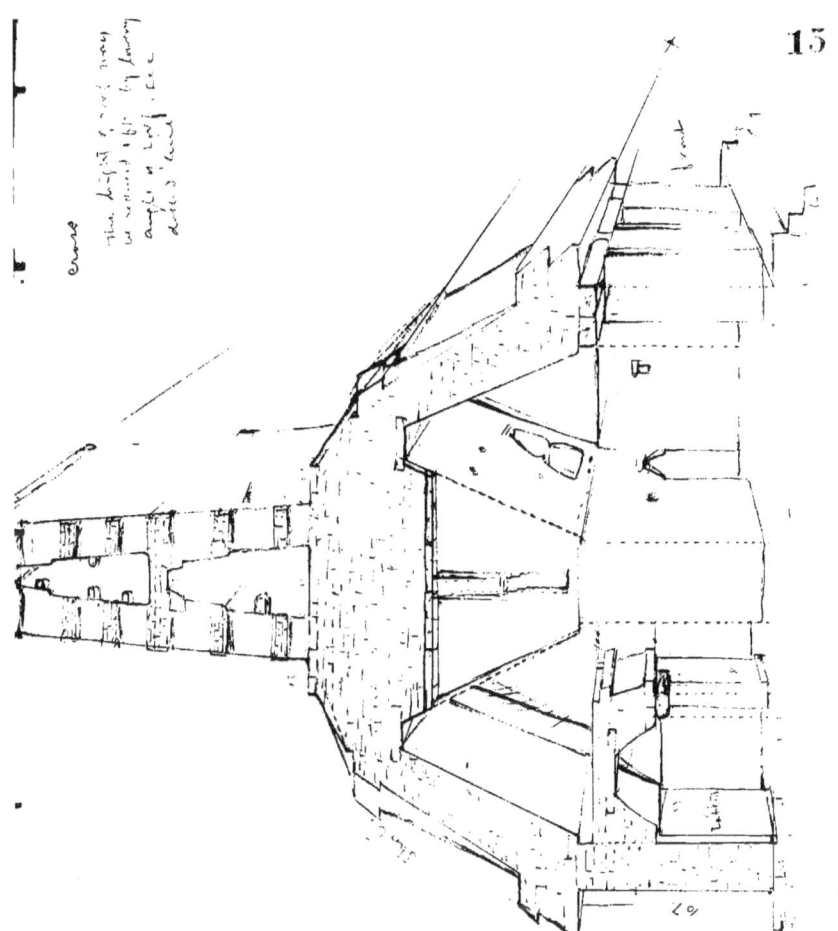

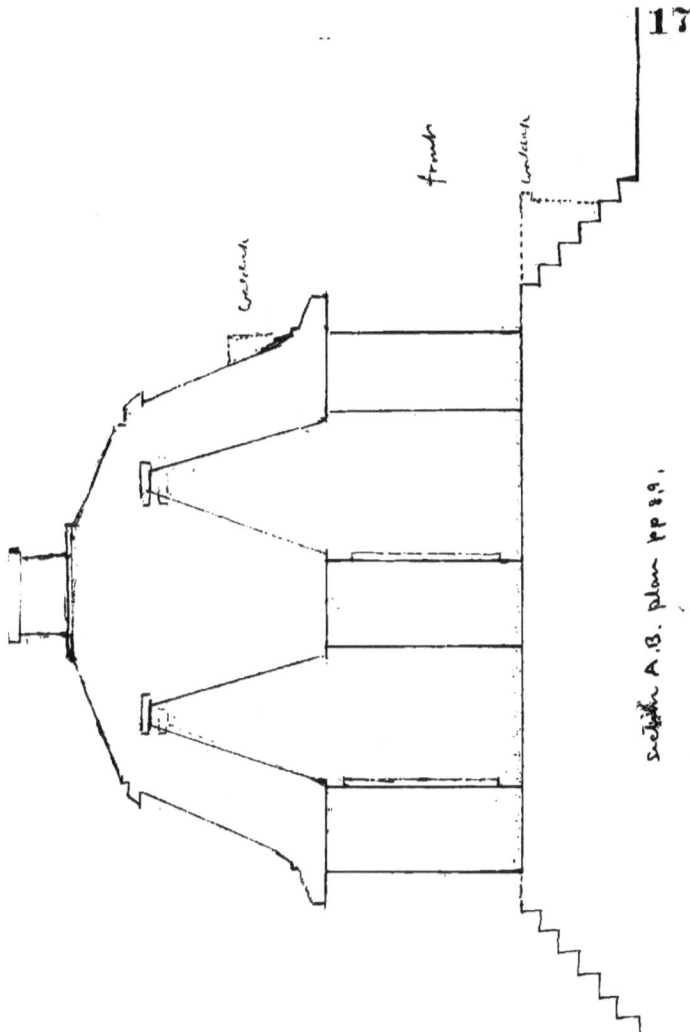

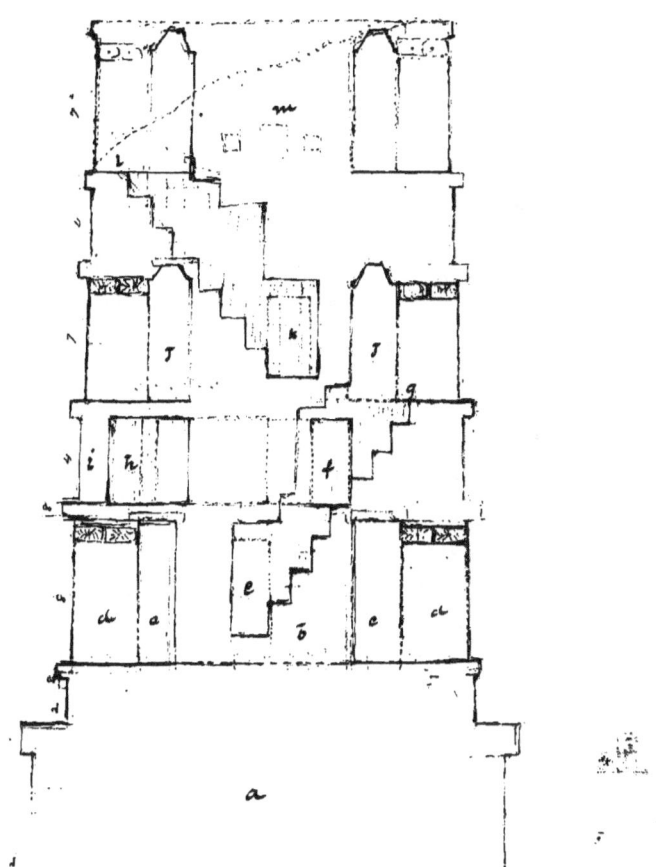

२३

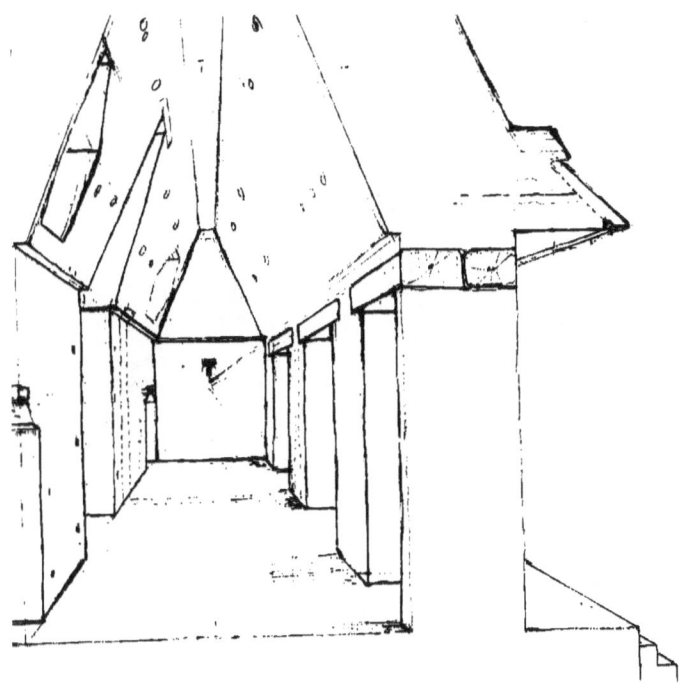

47

48

~~Shrines tend as above~~
~~cd—————————tabl~~
describe groups & figures & costumes
mention tgt of each tablet & Stephen [Expression]
sgd...

~~Describe...~~

~~Cord holders~~
Sunken Tablet ~~short board~~ ~~at Hunt~~
~~Floors of Court & boat~~

[sketch] side of door

[sketch of dots]

Del Rio
Du Paix
Waldeck
Kingsborough copies
Dupaix

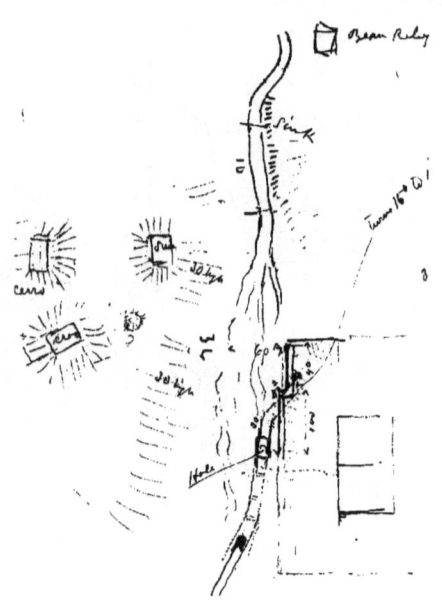

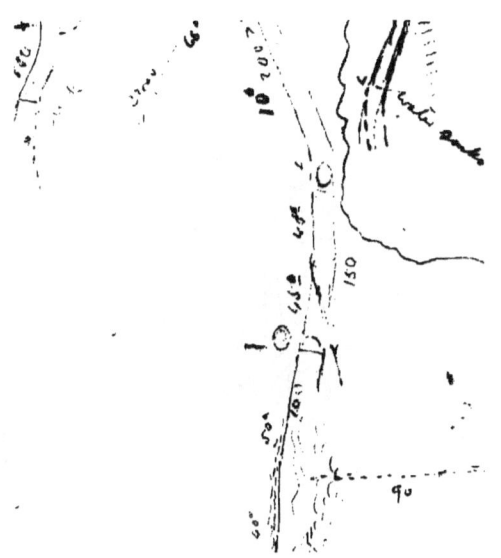

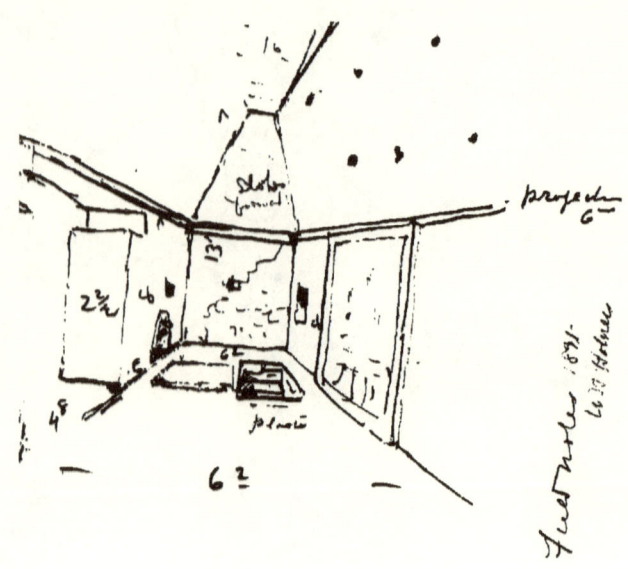

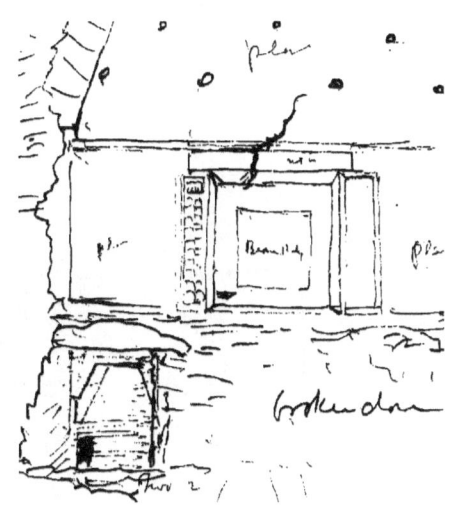

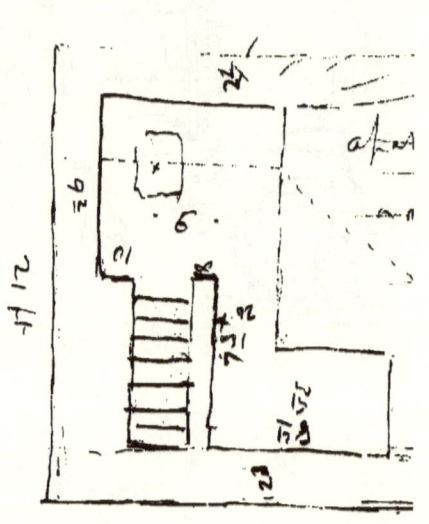
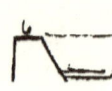

This masterpiece may be taken as a sample of the work of the old artists — stucco. A rough wall of irregular stones of smallish size was laid in plaster somewhat even, then plaster was applied perhaps an inch thick where work was to be done. If the relief was high bits of stone were set into the ground making a framework for the features. These were kept well within the outline and as the stucco was modeled these stones usually disappeared. Where strong features or members were to be set on, a shallow pit was dug in the wall as a socket for the projecting stone.
    Behind the right side of the figure is now a hole through the wall some 6 in square, probably nothing to do with the F's, at elbow. The modeling is bold, free and in forms of life, drapery & conventional ornament

~~being there hieroglyphs~~ are still nearly intact. The second from the top at left and the 3rd & 4th from below on the right, outlines ? others shown.

This Chac't legs are complete save part of a scroll leaf under the chin and the hind ~~tail~~. Surface is rough where the figure is pulled off showing the rude masonry in place.

The glyphs were molded and set into the wet plaster ~~surface~~. The animals & chacs were modeled in place. Coarser gravelly mortar at first on the stone then finer while underneath very like plaster of paris.

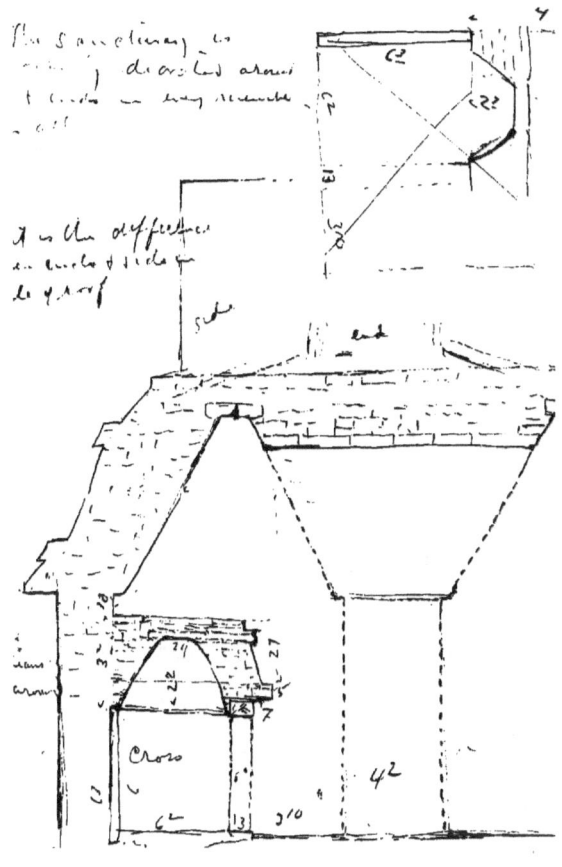

a no request I given
Fees q sanctuary place in
founders castle @ or 4
lluch + 6.16 × 3 = (?) L

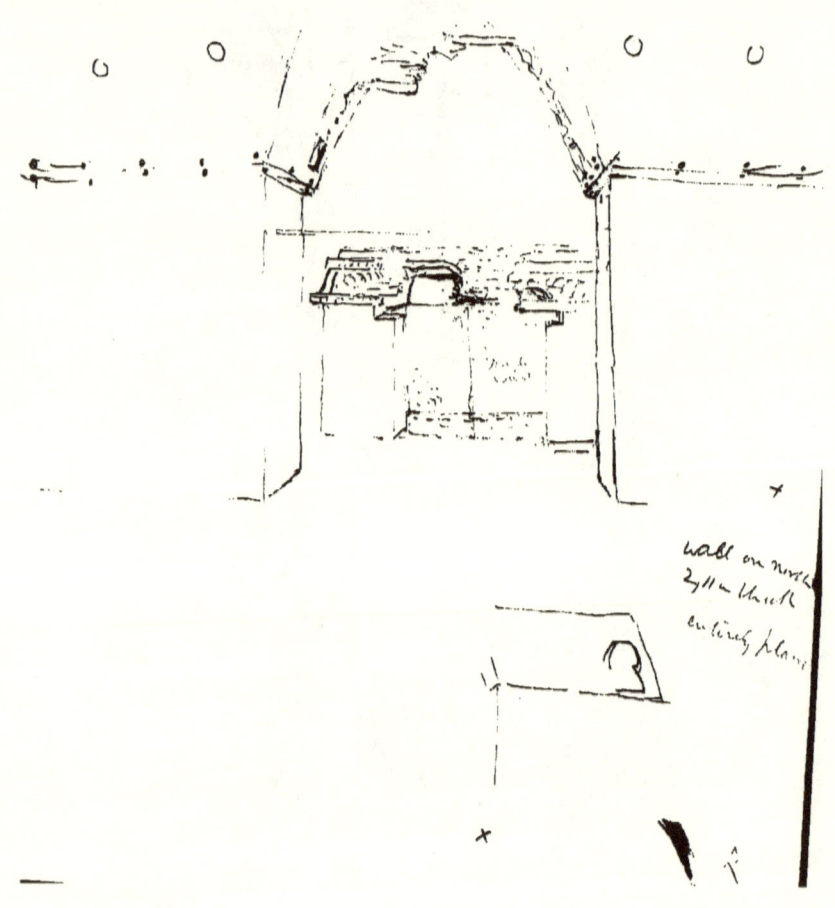

Palace

Appropriately enough called the palace as it is
most extensive and pretentious structure or
of structures in the ancient city.

a great [and] quadrangle of buildings
enclosing a pyramid

outer building or line of Bldgs is covered by a
and greater continuous + now partly fallen and
not 20ft wide and compresses two lines of ofter
or corridors, a central wall is bordered by
on either arches supporting outside + inside
[...]. This rectangle encloses several
[...] courts

1st The north half is independent [...]

Palace

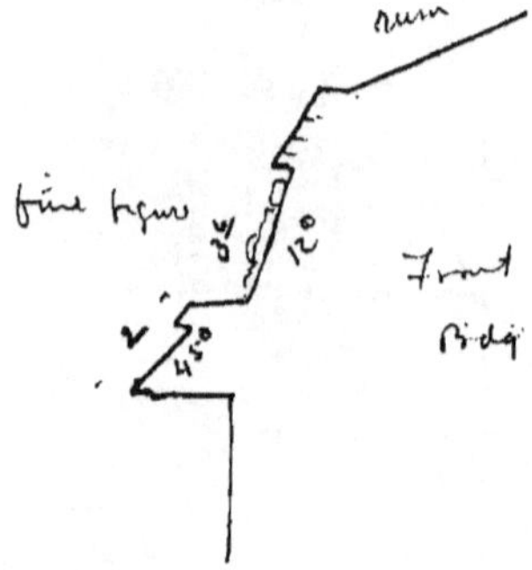

ruin

fine figure

45°
12°

Front Bldg south front palace
Bldg of the Reever Tan

ruin comb

12
20

fine stucco
6
12

12

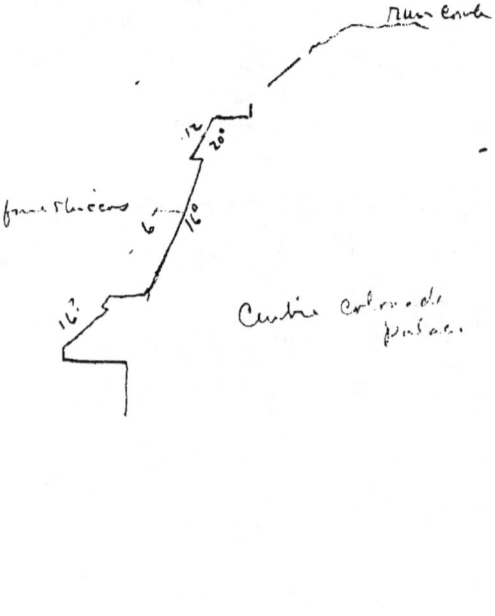

Centre Colonnade
palace

West Bdg.

- walls across corridor, late one moved cupld
  one for each pillar. Import recesses, deep about same
  as west corridor. Small end holes at all
  openings torches, several lines in pillars
  + wall, pillars long. Walls all plain, color
  crocs + some designs - painted one town
- Much deposit on all walls
- Kelumes in all inter-lintel spaces over groups

West court 7 small 6 ft high 1/2 brnt slab which is the
recessed around at north + one next lower
slabs 12 long at south on east side
one of few of tombs where there is a bit of carved
stone work

north pillars
"2 figs left part of setting - shield gone. also head
and hands (facing figs) right fig with right hand up
holding ax. final left (?) leg + part of other gone.
Glyphs nearly all gone. Colors
Beautiful decoration color

Cornice above nearly all gone.
Stair begins 2 ft out but is covered
4th arch from south fallen out 3 ft length
others less than 2 ft
Columns about 6 ft wide
South building beyond south glyph column well
down inner wall and arch slope left
Glyph column 6 ft face. inner wall of south
forms to middle
South end has door   End of arch on wall
                           and over door & has hole
                           about 15 wide 30 high

West corridor Complete save 2 ft N end
2 put holes alternate with 6 bufort recesses 6" 10"
deep on wall side of arch

small slow plastered ???

2 [tow?] holes down [toward?] door one little window
down within 8 ft of N End   wall well covered
with deposit over plaster — almost perfect
Outer arch slope has ? of these

looking west

West Bldg

West pillars all fine & plain Save the beautiful
stucco groups on the outside a D another row of fine
Glyphs on the south pillar 2 ft wide by about 6 ft high

b next north Standing figure right sitting left heads
& other parts gone , beautiful modeling , red &
Green colors still visible. fine arms & shoulder
on Standing figs. glyphs top left & bottom

c next north nearly all gone

d next north 2 standing figs. facing left face perfect
other ".gone.   height ... , modeling fine . 4 inches

e 4 1/2 half length chest & shoulders. part of right
  . gone , Red, blue, green colors. seen
  ... view of left side of face

f ornament at base

g fine figures at left leaning to right will have
  ... & kneeling fig under at right
  Great work with beautiful serpent designs & Katuns
  below glyphs all around , Head of left figure gone
  ... right arm & legs of kneeling , G human
  glyphs around about half gone

The west Bay is still intact save the roof & corner pillar at the N.W. from the 5th free pillar to the end of bdg proper - about 17 feet, and the west end of the north bdg. leaving the wall and its half of the arch to the corner complete; around the north this condition continues for forty feet when the arches [just?] descends, having fallen out leaving a great break outside in above and along line of pillars

Temple of the cerro

One of the finest of the three great Complex
Lintels.

Center gorgeous bird at top
Grotesque head with plumes many be bird face
Face gorget unbound
Cross links arms at shoulder
Glyphs at left below + superb flourish designs
belly lower third

Short young fig at right with glyphs in front
of face + above, 4 lines of glyphs at right
Splendid tall fig at left head with upthrown hair
arm long head-dress at top, grotesque face the
under feet hands with uplifted offering (grotesque small) + drapes
napkin on level of face.

Reposefully presume
Delicately + perfectly carved 1/4 to 3/8" deep
other wall all plain

[margin: August 7 under 2 from 1 20 ft]

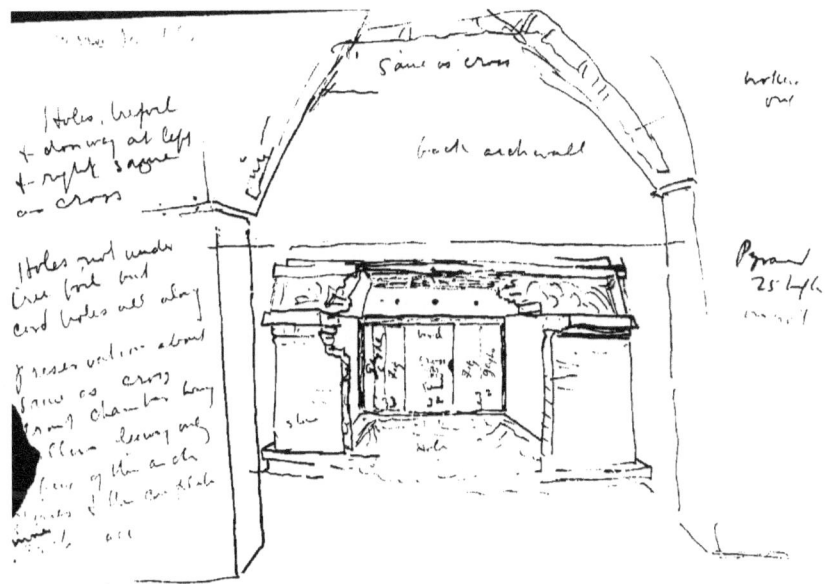

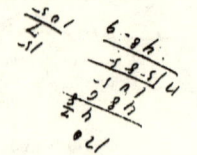

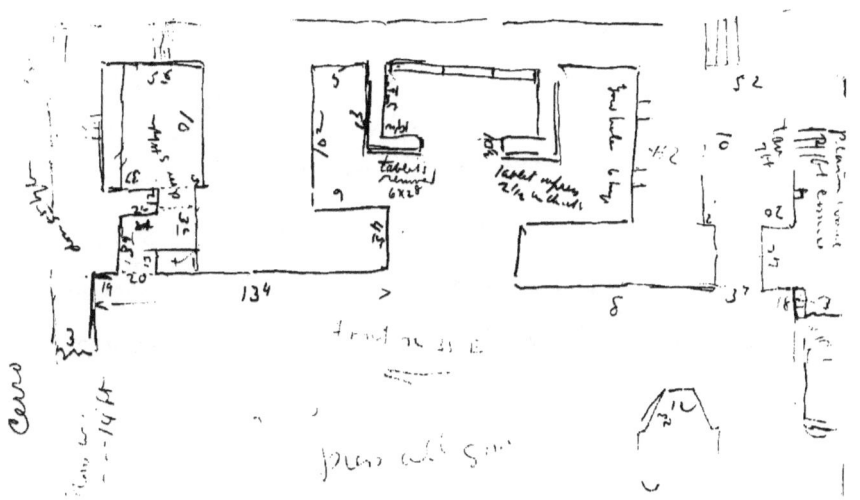

Inter-Court Bdg   Castle

This section is entire save wooden lintels of which there were 13 pans, none of the arches have fallen much over two feet — one about 3. The arches are now flat and secure the whole body of masonry masonry having been solidified by deposit. Plaster is still nearly complete. The stone facings of small and a very few medium to large — in all positions rough mat faces well rounded nearly whole, plaster up to 2 inches thick. Red paint in many places and in south and west side numerous traces of figures in blue + red. Geometric symbolic devices + figures.

Two figures or groups of figures in stucco on middle wall at south end, also traces on the in + s faces of several western pillars. 3 of the same type on middle pillars facing west are about half preserved, faces gone, others nearly all gone, very fine all equalling

Recent walls between some pillars 6 ft high – traces now seen only and recent because over stucco figure traces

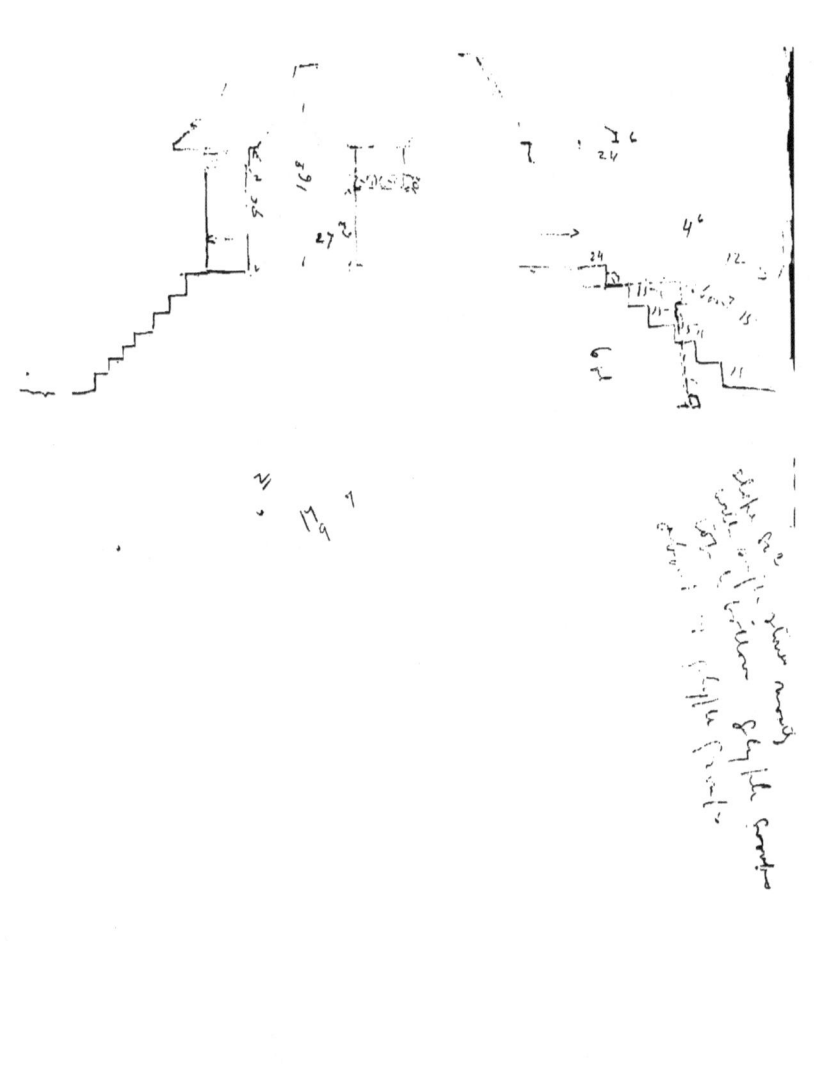

Outer wall 3ft 2in, pillars 2" thick
East corridor west wall has 9 grotesque faces near top [north west?] of door 9 ft south of n end 14 ft, all somewhat mutilated 3 nearly all gone
all grayish white in color a recent coat to plaster or cast. 3 Tau holes in the wall one at north end.
  Opening in east have been walled up with 1 ft wall to top, or nearly [leaves line?] at top of floor
  some remain 3 ft high
  Stucco figs all gone from east face pillars holding stones still seen + much red color, blue + other colors in plaster. beneath

Temple of the Sun

The three in place in the little inner temple with its piers rough as if figs had been post[?] its cornices & [?] in spots with extremes of [?] [?] the still in place. [?] of arch has destroyed middle[?] Inner chamber of tablets usual arch with three holes[?] holes, no tablets. Tablets perfect but [?] [?] and [?] with col, debs, sides plain plaster [?] [?] [?] figs but [?] coated. Two curtain holes at each side of front

Front arch good
about 20 length
  Grand arches

  Temple of Sun.

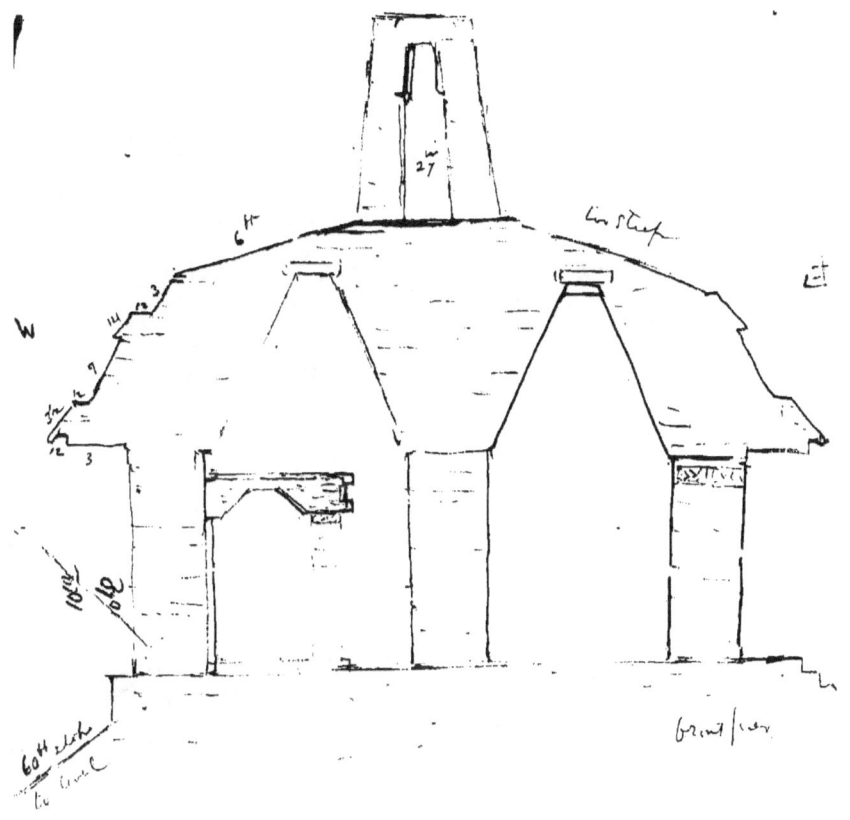

Temple of Croso from Temple
Feb. 8th 98

K.
arrow
point

This small Bldg is still well preserved
½ the roof being complete and the central arch
standing well along. One inner pier - north w
broken down (out of way) — some outer arch
3 from north stand half, but 2 + the corner
pier are gone. The inner wall and the whole
string of the arches are complete + some of the
cap stones are in place even where the
outer + inner piers + arch-side have fallen.
The inner north end of the arch is still
intact

<u>Centre wall</u>
        Plain inside with four Tau holes
+ 6 great hinge bolts at sides of great
archway. This is the grandest + most
perfect of the arches with square opening below
+ true foil arch. 3 trefoil pannels on either
side — arch slopes
7 Bust rosettes at left 6 at right heads
all gone, necks + shoulders remain. The innate

East Bay 2

framework - a slightly squared circle with
deep line and [illegible] [illegible] [illegible]
in high relief. Grotesque [illegible] heads
at four corners. Natives & [illegible] like figs & flourishes
Any rest 4 ft space along top, 20 ft at N, and
quite plain [illegible] at South wall. [illegible] Bdy. well down
the outer frieze & all the arch & top gone

Medallions all have been richly handled
in 2 reds, blue, green, yellow

Outside frieze
[illegible crossed out] [illegible] have super-
[illegible] northern [crossed out] gone, fine fig with batan
face south, sitting fig at his [illegible] [illegible]
sitting figure behind face & [illegible]

+ head of [illegible] [illegible], otherwise nearly perfect
+ elbow
mouth of latter border part gone, left feature
nose
above OK.

2nd Bay

4th bay from south
  like 5th but two extra tops + border
  among gone, 2 right Kahuna[?] perfect
  lower front of face of standing fig gone

3rd pier ("Chamay")
  Same group of 3. Standing fig faces all
  face gone, also face of right sitting fig.
  Standing fig has halo.
  3 Kahunas above perfect. Sides gone.

2nd pier. Same group. Stand. fig [?],
  with face + hands gone. Below pier
  other figs perfect. L/hos hall Kahuna

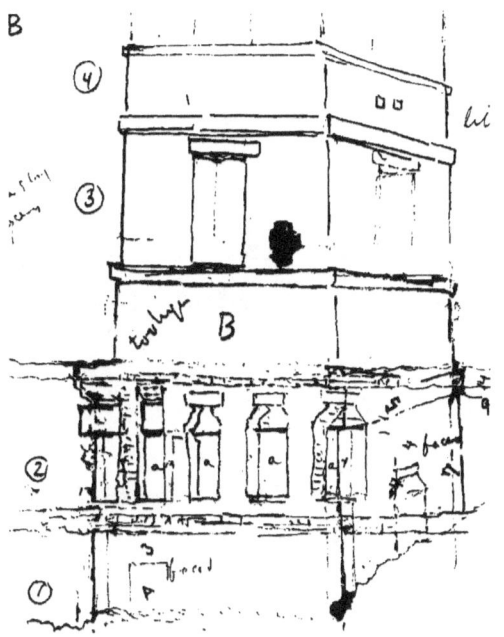

near middle of house
arranged about a tau

next room yes has [?] much [?]
around a tau
also fuller figures [?] others an

squat big of oval tabled has some fine [?]
and pendant emblematic [?] in 1st,
the south room, a long gallery has it
in the east wall + some [?] [?]

much [?] curved + [?] over paneled,
— red + black above

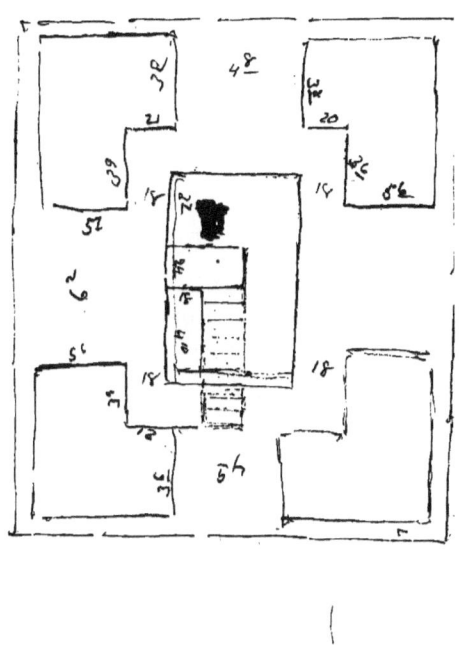

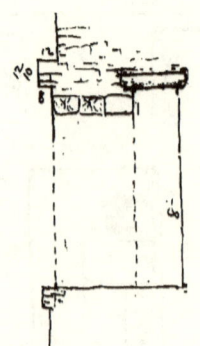

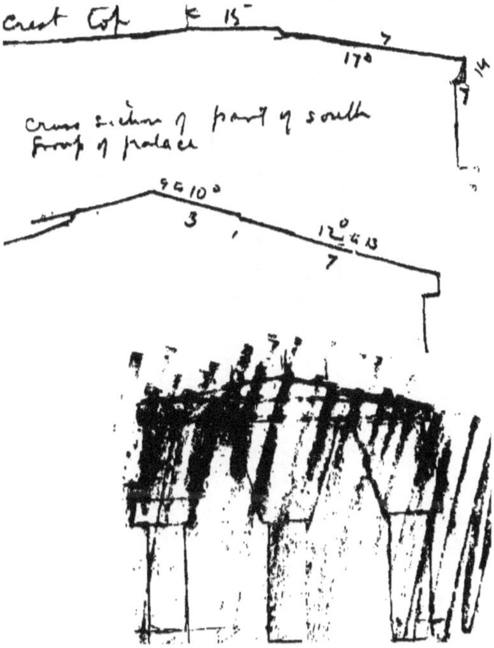

Crest top |← 15 →| 7
                    17°   14
                             7

Cross section of part of south
front of palace

         4 & 10°
            3   12° & 13
                     7

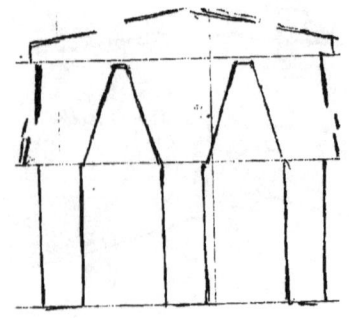

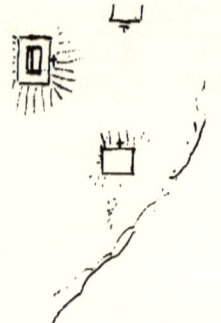

~~and~~ but we cannot at present
say whether the facings were of stone ~~or~~ or plaster

Fig. 4

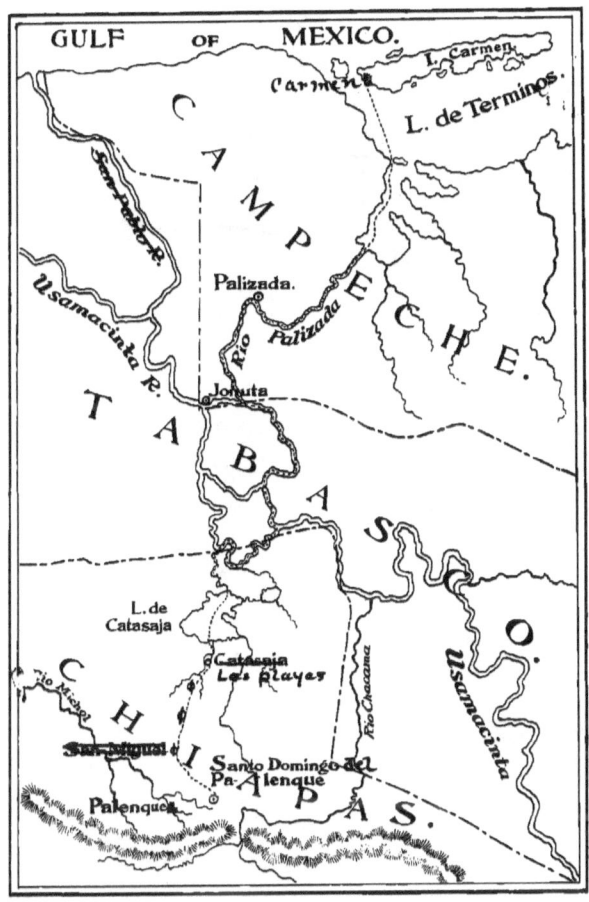

3 Le Petits

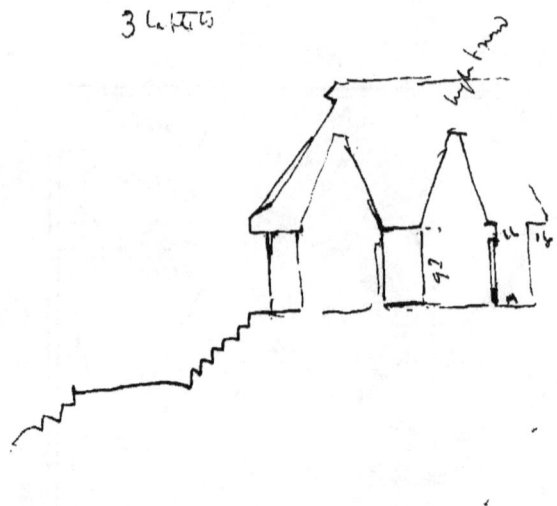

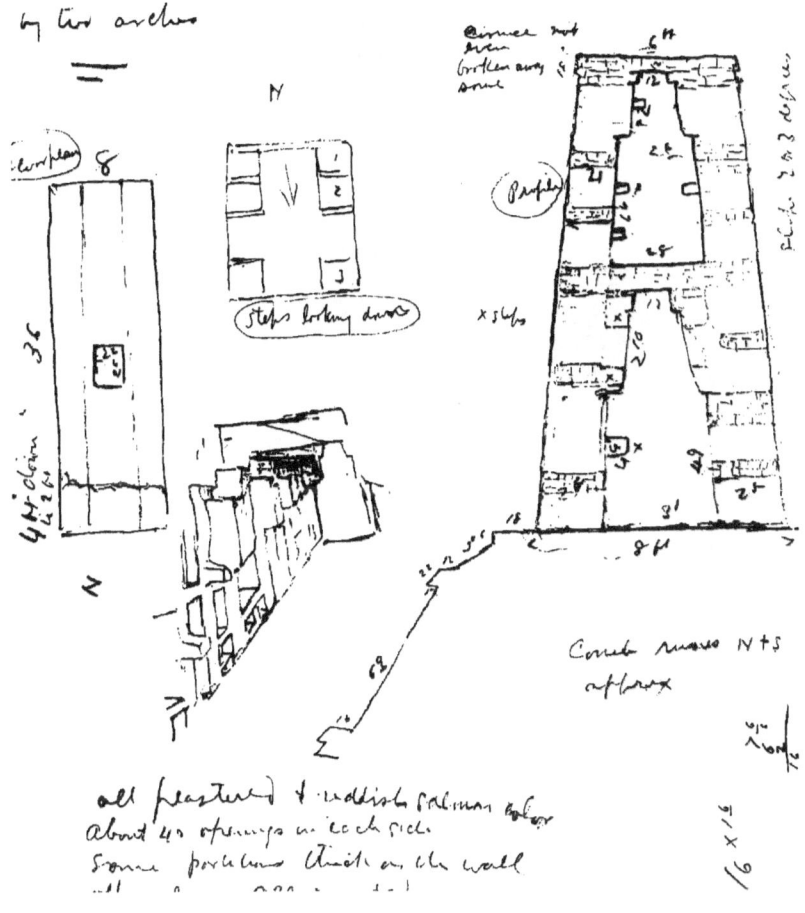

324

' 61

north end of palace.
— down
+any. stand 40 ft at west and watch
= east. rest. is all below spring of arch
of same

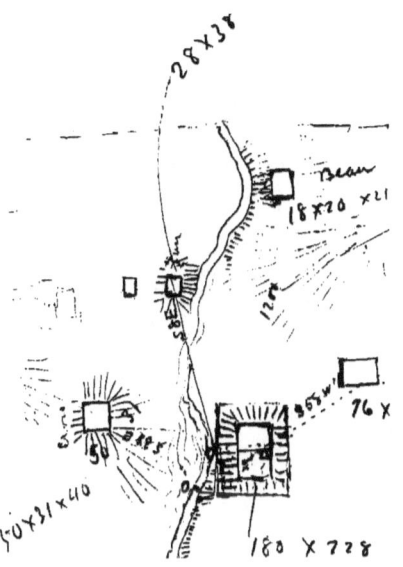

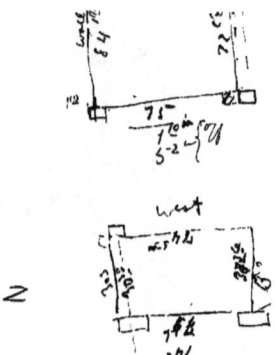

elevern, [strikethrough] long 7 feet wide. Their height to the lintel sockets is 8 feet and the entablature moulding and cornice the spring of the arch — see section 9 feet. The slope of the arch inclines appears to be a little less. Above that of the entablature without so that the masonry thickens upward. The medial mass of masonry, between the arches and extending upward in the roof [vaults?] is extremely ponderous. The [strikethrough] archways through the medial wall, are [height?] and of peculiar construction [strikethrough] above & their [strikethrough] [strikethrough]. There are but three of these preserved, one through the [north?] range, one [thigh?] " " South

pierced by some 40 or 50 wall openings being represented only by the piers. Both arches are included under a single roof which consists of an outer steep slope, nearly ~~[illegible]~~ the entablature of the facade, an upper slope pit at at a low angle and a low roof-comb in the centre.

The exterior piers are somewhat uniformly spaced but the interior openings are varied to suit the courts or blank walls which they face.

A typical section is given in Fig X showing p.

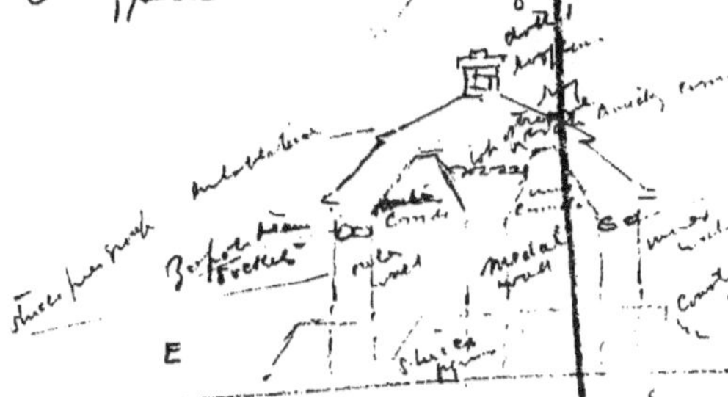

E

Fig x section of one of the Palace buildings

Details of masonry. The interior structures of the South division show variations of this principle, the entablature facade being vertical in one case and the lower rises nearly vertically 4 stones.

on the S S Court contains a on
ding, centrally placed, the S dis. Coo
rooms near the north and and a
and apartments at the south end

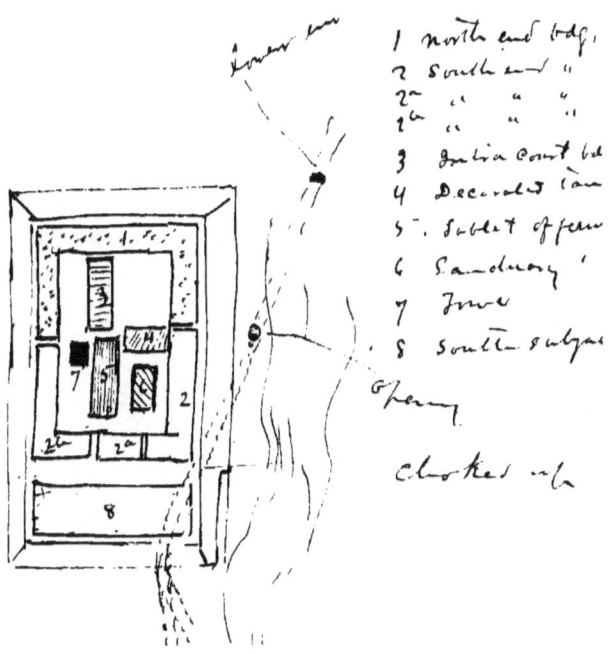

1 north end bdg.
2 South end "
2ᵃ " " "
2ᵇ " " "
3 Julia Court bd
4 Decorated ?
5ᵗ. Sublet of pew
6 Sanctuary '
7 Tower
8 South subject

Opening

Choked up

I saw no columns in Palenque. Their place is taken by flattish piers which are nothing more that sections of the normal wall left (as supports for the Entablature) between the entrance-ways. These piers are however, a constant and important feature of the buildings, extending entirely around the palace and bordering its courts and presenting the only exterior variation of the monotonous facades of the temples.

    Gables
    Windows ?

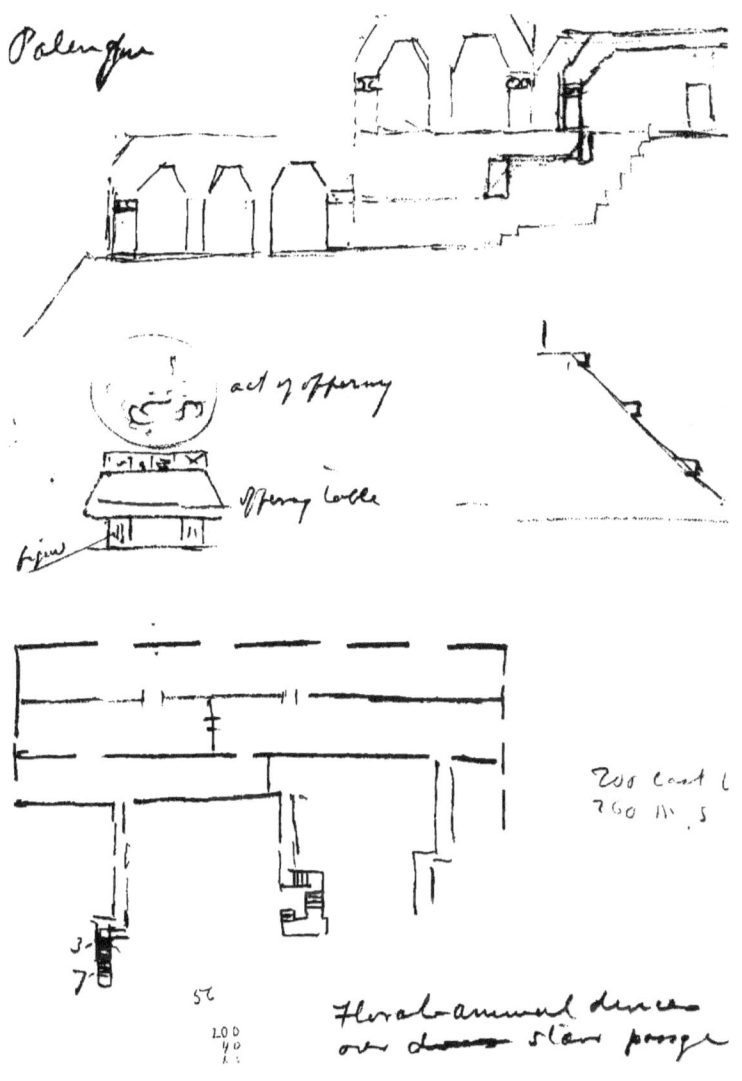

and the sides abutting against the hill
the ground in front level.

76 a

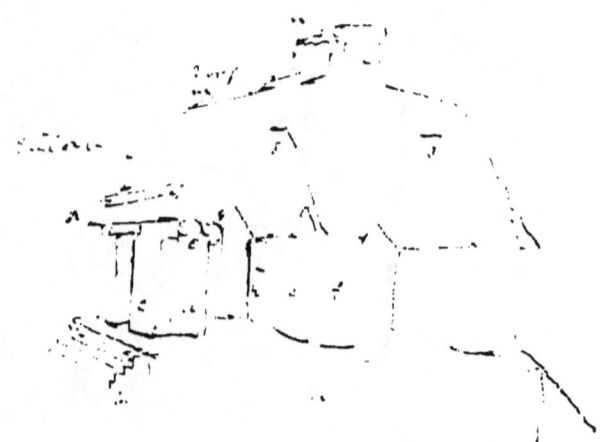

www.ingramcontent.com/pod-product-compliance
Lightning Source LLC
Chambersburg PA
CBHW022132160426
43197CB00009B/1245